MW01483859

RELIGION:

WHO NEEDS IT?

By
Nasir Makr Hakim
(Minister of Elijah Muhammad, Messenger of Allah)

Published by
Secretarius MEMPS Publications
111 E Dunlap Ave, Ste 1-217
Phoenix, Arizona 85020-7802
Phone & Fax 602 466-7347
Email: secmemps@gmail.com
Web: www.memps.com

RELIGION: WHO NEEDS IT?

ISBN 1-884855-02-4
978-1-884855-02-3

Printed in the United States of America

DEDICATION

To all the Believers and Followers
of
Elijah Muhammad,
Messenger of Allah,
without whom, we as fractions
would have no expectation
of ever
becoming whole.

~ ~ ~ ~ ~

The
Messenger
is a Sword
In A Man's Hand

~ Sayings of Elijah Muhammad, Vol. 3

TABLE OF CONTENT

RELIGION: Who Needs It?

RELIGION: WHO NEEDS IT?

Historically, religion, aside of land, has been one of the most prevailing reasons for which wars have been fought. When reflecting back approximately 6,000 years, this fact can be supported easily.

Religion as well has been used to exploit whole races and nations of people around the world. Its negative effect has been so drug-like, that it's being widely considered by many as the "Opium" of the masses.

One aspect is quite interesting and that is, regardless of the religion, it seems that the gods in them all favors white or light colored people, especially if you use the progress of nations as the measuring stick. They seem to bestow more progress and tend to extend more "blessings." They tend to shed greater levels of power and advancements of civilization than what aboriginal gods bestow, so it seems.

Whether it's the Buddhists and their yellow looking gods, the Hindus and their light-colored brown looking gods, the white Arabs or the white Christians and their blonde-haired, blue-eyed "Jesus," if one were to quickly take a world panoramic view, where is a "successful" black nation under any of the above "gods?" One must ask, how far out of the loop are we? Must we serve as step-children in any circumstance we find ourselves? Why is not there a God that looks like us?

RELIGION: WHO NEEDS IT?

Of the above, the aboriginals of the earth, not in just one geographical location, has suffered tremendously under white Christians, than any of the above that remain. But the question about religion still remains: Who needs it?

DEFINITION: SETTING THE TERMS OF REFERENCE

According to Webster's II, New Riverside University Dictionary, the word "religion" means: Belief in and reverence for a supernatural power accepted as the creator and governor of the universe. The word comes from the Latin: Religio (reverence, piety, dutifulness) and from the French: Religore (to tie back, tie up, tie fast), and lastly from the Archaic: scrupulous conformity. All the above definitions are important as you will come to see.

The definition starts off by saying there is a belief in and reverence for a supernatual power. As the Creator (God) has created the whole creation soley by Himself and it is considered the only expression like it known to man, and is considered the ULTIMATE NORMALITY, so much so, it's called the "NATURAL ORDER." Why would there exist something else that's considered "Super" natural? Isn't this like saying "Pre-historic." As the Honorable Elijah Muhammad, Messenger of Allah, points out, that the first law of creation is motion and motion is the definition of time and the making of time is history; therefore, what was before time, which could qualify for the term "Pre-historic" or "pre-time?"

To even pursue going after what was before time, is to actually be asking what was before God? The Messenger teaches us that while the Creator was creating himself, definition also was being created then. There was nothing qualifying for a definition. Thus, the word nothing. This word carries the idea of that which is making no time, that which occupies no space, that which does not exists according to the definition of the Author of Existence. This definition was established after the Creator created himself, then the definition was established.

As a result of rotating for trillions of years in the darkness, this process, in and of itself, is now used by the creator as a process which all life coming into His creation must undergo. As the Messenger put it, "A little small atom of life rolling around in darkness. Think over it: Building itself up, just turning in darkeness, making its own self...He made Himself into total darkness. He put His Ownself turning, turning on His

Own Timetable in the Black womb of the Universe. He started rotating. He demands every life that comes into the Universe today to start turning firse. 'Over to Me, for I had that to do myself.' "Now, I am going to see that every life that comes into this Universe comes out of total darkness - every life!" (OSHA, pg. 43)

FORM DICTATES FUNCTION

This lays the basis for all that came afterwards. In other words, once the creator created a thing, it was given value based on it's function and form. Its whole purpose for existing was solely based on it's function. That is what locked in and substantiated its definition. The definition is what its value is based on, and within the purpose lays the definition. As long as a thing is functioning according to the purpose for which it was created, then it is earning or justifying the right to continue existing. We're talking place value here. This is what zeros are for, holding a place (smile).

"Turning over to Me," is a very essential aspect here, because when we look into the definition of the term, universe, etymologically, we see "Uni" and "Verse." According to the Latin, "uni" means "one," and "verse," according to the Latin means "to turn." Notice the way the planets rotate and the consequential aspect of it when it comes to how we as humans exists. This planet's turning towards the sun is one essential element responsible for gravity, our oxygen, blood pressure, etc... Therefore, this "turning" especially in one direction is in fact the only reality we know and have all but forgotten about it, considering we have grown so accustomed to it. The turning in one direction have become so common-place that we just refer to it as being the "natural" order of things, nature, but is it everyone's nature and is it natural to everyone?

There is nothing greater than the created reality. We as humans have been born out of it and have come to know it as such. The "Natural" is the most super expression of existence we will ever experience. What could possibly make it appear super to us perhaps is our ignorance of what the total natural expression is. A crawling baby becomes excited when it walks for the first time, because to always be watching adults come and go so fast, with so much ease, makes them think what we are doing is super, but that disipates once they start walking then after a few weeks or month, they forget all about it, and the "super naturalness" of walking becomes "normal."

Notice as well that within Webster's definition, it says that it not only meant a belief in the "supernatural," but that this "supernatural" power had to be "accepted" as the creator and governor of the universe.

Belief is defined as a mental condition or habit of placing trust or confidence in a person or thing. Supernatural generally relates to and is commonly accepted as something which exists outside of the natural world - something "miraculous, insubstantial or illusory." Therefore, we see here that religion is a mental conditioning or habit of placing trust or confidence in a power or something outside of the natural world. A belief in that which is other than the natural law or the process which the creator established. I know that some of you smart ones are already peeping into where I am going. I ask for you endulgence.

ONE MAN & SIN

As we are coming to see, the element of ORDER is a key and essential element to the functioning and defining of this creation, natural order or created reality, then the question rises, what term is used to illustrate or articulate that which is contrary or opposed to order.

Given the context we are traveling in, religion is the context from which we will attempt to solicit an answer. In the context of religion, sin is the term most associated with going against or going contrary to God's order or law - although we know, not just believe - that it's the natural law, order, nature, etc... Most often religious people use the term sin to illustrate the process or the results of one transgressing the law or the rules governing God's order.

Sin is transgression of the law - what law? Many have been short-stopped right there, because of hiding the truth on the white man's part and ignorance on the part of many so-called Negro preachers. The law in question has always been the Creator's law. What law did the Creator set up? He set up natural law and that law was and still is sufficient to govern His creation. How would we recognize His law? It is His words in Motion, which is why in the Book of St. John, chapter 1, one will see it said that in the beginning was the Word. And since Allah, the Creator of the Heavens and the Earth, sets His universe in motion, the direction changes Not. The Word "Uni," which comes from the Latin: Unus, meaning one, and the word verse, comes from the

RELIGION: WHO NEEDS IT?

Latin: vertere, meaning to turn. This Creation, which God has Created only turns one direction and the order, laws and principles upon which it turns never changes. All this is considered Natural Law and Order, and when one violates, conflict with or tries to operate outside of it, one is sinning.

Now, what's worth pondering is that which is said in the Book of Romans (Bible); wherein, it states, "By one man sin entered into the world." Therefore, a good question would be: Before that "One Man" what was the world like? It was in order, concord, peace and paradise, or heavean as we refer to it. In fact, whole kingdoms and societies existed on that basis. This is why the Bible talked about paradise, heaven and the garden.

So, from whence came the peace breaking, hell, and the need for a religion? What creature created within the creation would long for something outside of its own "natural" circumstance, its own existence? How would it know if something existed outside of its existence? Don't forget this question; it is the basis of all deception. Transgressing or going against natural law was started by one man.

Both the Bible and Holy Qur'an teaches us of a time and the end of a time when God, Himself would come, and we would see Him as He Is. A very pivitol and essential aspect to this would be that His Last Messenger would have to come first. The scripture also tells of the name, works and characteristics of this last one. Elijah Muhammad fits the description of what we were to expect. How this is so is not the subject of this book; however, these aspects are dealt with in detail in the two compilation of Elijah Muhammad's work called, <u>The True History of Master Fard Muhammad</u>, and <u>The Black Stone: The True History of Elijah Muhammad</u>.

Messenger Elijah Muhammad taught us that Almighty Allah, (God) Came and made His appearance in the Person of Master Fard Muhammad, as it was prophesied throughout Biblical as well as Qur'anic scripture. He taught us what Allah would do in the last days, and that Allah revealed to him the knowledge of just who that one man is.

He taught us that this man produced a people who were pure sin on two feet. This is not a people who merely contracted or are infected with sin, no. This is a people who are sin in the flesh. This man's name is Yakub (his history is in greater detail in Messenger Elijah Muhammad's book, Message To The Blackman In America). One can read his history in Biblical and Qur'anic scripture as well. In the Bible his name is translated as Jacob and in the Qur'an, as Iblis.

To institutionalize something is to organize it in such a way as to make it self-sustaining, able to reproduce itself, protect itself and perpetuate itself long after the founder is gone. With the process of institutionalized birth control, Mr. Yakub was able to take 59,999 black people on an island called patmos (pelan in the Bible), off the Agean sea near the country of Greece and produce, over a period of 600 years, a completely grafted man and woman from the Black man. This process resulted in the end product looking like it had no color at all - "a bleached" human, so to speak.

AND YE SHALL KNOW THEM BY THEIR WORKS

Producing this new people through the process of grafting is symbolized in the Bible under the story of Jacob wrestling with an angel until the break of day and although he had a hard time, as it is symbolized by wrestling, he prevailed, but before he prevailed, he had made the angel with whom he wrestled, give him something - a name change for his product or people; which as well served as their definition, as well as their cover or veil for a time. In the 28th verse of the 32 chapter of Genesis, the angel took the name Jacob and gave them the name Israel. All white folk came from the same root and father, as Jesus pointed out in his discourse with the Jews starting in St. John 8:32-45. All white folks are "Israel" and they have been robbing the Black peoples of the knowledge of their true history by impersonating them as God's chosen, who in essence are the real "devils" and not the chosen of God .

The story of their history started with the symbolic story of Adam and Eve. That is the Genesis or beginning of white people, not black people. This is why it's so easy for them to say "pre-historic," because the black people had history, not them; they had just started 6,000 years ago. These people are made in "Our" image and after "Our" likeness. That's why they look like us. They are not Original like you and I; this is why we and they refer to themselves as "man-kind." They are a "kind" of a man, but not Original like you and I.

So, since we understand now what is meant by, "as by one man sin entered into the world," what is this supernatural power they have accepted as god, and how have they been able to use it on the natural man until this late date?

Previously we discovered that the definition of religion was, "A belief in and reverence for a supernatural power accepted as the creator and governor of the universe." The earliest recorded or archaic definition: scrupulous conformity. Clarity of this definition is important, because without which, it dooms the entire article to misunderstanding.

The definition was taken from Webster's II, New Riverside University

Dictionary and as we carefully examine it, we will see some key words such as "supernatural" and "accepted." These words are pointed out to illustrate a point. If the Creator created this universe, which is not exceeded by anything known to man, and its laws and principles which govern it are so constant and transcending that it is universally considered "Natural," what would be considered "super-natural?" The bottom line is that whatever it is referred to as supernatural, it is actually referring to something considered outside of the natural order of the universe, and the word "super" is put on it to shield or hide the deception and concealed the fact that what's being passed off as something greater, is really a trick, inticement or inducement for the unsuspecting to accept something which is in essence contrary to nature or the natural order of this creation.

The name Israel refers not to one man or one state in the middle east, but symbolically to all of the products which came as a result of the grafting of one man, which is why all white people are Israel, not just the ones in occupying Palestine. The process symbolized by the wrestling was a grafting process which took place on the Island of Pelan or Patmos in the Aegean Sea, off the coast of Greece, the cradle of white civilization. The grafting process, in short, produced a bleached black man and woman and this is what made them a kind of a man, not an original, but MAN-KIND.

You may reflect on the argument between Jesus and the Jews in the Bible, John 8:32-44 versus, about whose father was whose. Jesus stated there that they were from their father, the devil. This also shows that Messenger Elijah Muhammad wasn't the first to call whites devils. Jesus did and proved it 2,000 years ago and the devil's own history has supported these facts to date; additionally, as Jesus said they were devils, then if he was a Jew, or the king of the Jews, as the devil translators added, he would in fact have been calling himself a devil too, because on numerous occasions, Jesus would reference "The Father." If he made a distinction between the Jew's father as the devil and his as God, surely they are not of the same parentage. Don't take my word for it, read the Bible, St. John 8:32-44.

The "supernatural power" they have "accepted" is a power which is not necessarily "super," but it is however outside of the natural power and is only considered "super" to the ignorant or those unaware of what the natural power is. This power is the science of tricks, which their father taught them to use on the Original people, to master them.

The whites know who God is, but they know most people don't know; therefore, they use the common people's ignorance against them by surrounding and astounding the common man with their representation of the world and racing with the natural order trying to show that they can do better. In their futile effort, they are destroying everything natural they put their hands on, from the water, air, land, space, the ocean, the people, the insects, the animals, plants and the very thinking of the peoples of the planet earth, and reaching for peoples on other planets.

The whites are natural corrupters, because they are not a natural people; they are a made people who have only been on the earth for only 6,000 years. The Adam and Eve referred to in the beginning of the Bible isn't talking about all peoples, just the beginning of whites. They were made in the original man and woman's image and after their likeness. This is why they look like us, not like a spirit, for spirits have no form!

When Adam's son Cain killed his brother Abel and then was banished, whose daughter did he find when traveling through the villages? It couldn't have been his sister (Adam's daughter, for Adam had no daughter), so whose daughter was it then? It was another peoples' female offspring, which is to point out that whites weren't on this planet first. To help us understand who was the first, why not go back to that natural order and law which the Creator created in the Beginning, which does not change.

Biology, chemistry and genetics, to name a few irrefutable laws which cannot be changed by man-kind, proves that a caucasian (white) man and woman can only reproduce a white child, but a Blackman and woman can produce every color in the spectrum which proves beyond a doubt that the black had to be the first, for whites can only produce whites, which means they were last. The Blackman and woman are the original peoples of the universe and are actually the direct descendants of the Creator Himself, which makes them gods, children of the Most High God, so teaches the Messenger of Allah (God), the Honorable Elijah Muhammad.

Whites know these truths, but they know we don't know. This is why they teach you and I that God is a spirit and can't be seen, because they know that if they teach you that God can't be seen, you will never look for Him. And as a result of slavery, they know the last place you and I will look for God will be in the mirror! It is this great trick and its maintenance, which keeps them ruling all the darker peoples of the Earth and they will continue to rule until their secret is revealed. The hiding of this secret is the whole basis to their secret societies.

As well as revealing all the above knowledge, the Honorable Elijah Muhammad, Messenger of Allah, also teaches us that after the father of the white race, Yakub, taught the white race how to graft themselves, because Yakub only lived for about 150 years, he told them to return to the Holy Land, Mecca, or the Garden of Eden, as it's called in the Bible, and go among the unsuspecting, peaceful people, and to sow discord, lies, and deceit among them. When the devils had put one brother against another, they would offer to settle their arguments for them and upon the original people allowing the devils to serve as mediators (like today's United Nations) the devils could rule them both. This process went on for six months until the devils turned the Holy Land upside down. After six months, the King had ordered that all the devils that "they could find" be rounded up and be stripped of everything except the language, and put on an apron to hide their nakedness, and made to walk over 22,000 miles across the desert, into the caves of West Asia, which we now call

Europe (Eu means caves and hillsides and rope was the rope to bind them in).

They went savage in the caves, which, by the way, is why there were no black cave people. Our fathers ran them into the caves, "across the burning sands." They lived there for 2,000 years until our fathers sent Musa (Moses) to them. Not in Egypt, but in the caves of Europe. They don't know their earlier history which is why they try to steal the early Black Egyptian's history with a white Cleopatra and the like.

ALLAH GIVE JUSTICE TO ALL

Upon them being found and civilized again, to enable them to come among civilized society once again, they had to undergo a study from 35 - 50 years in order to learn and do like the original man and are called Moslem Sons, and wear the Greatest Flag of the Universe, the Sun, Moon and Star, which fly higher than any flag in existence and has been flying since the creation itself. But, they had to have a sword on the upper part of the flag, which symbolized Justice, whereas, any time they revealed the secret, their head would be taken off by the sword. The head here represents rulership and their capacity to keep the people believing that God is somewhere in the sky and the devil is somewhere beneath the earth with fire and all that natural gas and gasoline products (smile).

The whites are the ones who need religion. If the black man is left alone, he would act natural, but considering we were kidnapped and robbed of the knowledge of even knowing ourselves, we don't know that we don't know ourselves; consequently, we "accept" the devils' definition of freedom and have become content with slavery in a mental form, thinking we're free. They believe in a power that is considered super to us, because we don't know any better, and we don't know our own. They have never let us be exposed to a world other than the one they have produced for us; therefore, we have no world to compare this one to. It has been said that, "He who gives you the diameter of your knowledge, prescribes the circumference of your activity."

So, since the whites taught us his language, history, sociology, psychology, and everything else, we see like he sees, but there is a difference, we still belong to the Creator and it is prophesied that He would come in the last days to seek and to save that which is lost. This is why the Qur'anic and Biblical scripture teaches of a time when there would be a resurrection of the dead, not a physically dead people, because, once again that would contradict the natural order of things, but a resurrection of a "mentally" dead people, who are in the "house of Israel." Not "OF" the house of Israel, but "IN" the house.

You and I don't need religion, we need to be taught back into our natural names, language, culture, God and Knowledge of Self. The white man needed an external aide, because it wasn't in him naturally. One doesn't have to teach and prod a bee to make honey or to beat and constantly remind a natural man to say his prayer - like white Arabs have to be. No, a natural being will do these things on his or her own. This is what is considered a continual prayer: their whole life is that of righteousness - naturally. It is time for the Blackman and Woman to accept their own, which is the whole planet, and to be themselves, which is a righteous Muslim. This is defined as one who submits their will to do the Will of God. "Are there any Muslims other than righteous, I beg your pardon, I have never heard of one." To say, there is no such thing as an unrighteous Muslim.

RELIGION: WHO NEEDS IT?

The Holy Qur'an says, "So set thy face for religion, being upright, the nature make by Allah in which He created men. There is no altering Allah's creation. This is the right religion - but most people know not. (HQ 30:30)

RELIGION: WHO NEEDS IT?

Made in the USA
Columbia, SC
18 February 2023

12637783R00026